Options Trading Strategies for Beginners

Table of Contents

Trading can be a pleasant method to make quick money. Investing, on the other hand, usually entails lesser short-term gains but also fewer significant losses.

This book includes all investing and trading options strategies for beginners to earn passive income. This guide will help you when, why, and how to invest and get a handsome amount.

CHAPTER 1

Introduction and criteria for investing

There are numerous investment options for new and enthusiastic investors to put their money in various projects and generate profits in the investing market. Many of them prefer to invest in various sorts of securities, including stocks, bonds, mutual funds, debentures, and so on, to maximize their profits.

On the other hand, Options trading might be one of the best investment opportunities for increasing your net worth. If you're a beginner who wants to work from home and invest in various sorts of options, you'll need to establish the following investing characteristics.

Here are the Criteria for Successful Investing

- Patience
- Perseverance
- Knowledge
- Honesty
- Pre-planning
- Discipline

Patience

Making a lot of cash in the markets is one of the most exciting professional experiences you can have. It has been accomplished in two ways, both yielding thousands of percent increases. The first was most likely a matter of luck rather than judgment. The latter was accomplished by employing abilities it takes a long time to learn. Allow yourself plenty of time to come up with a strategy. You get to the point where you're one with the markets and only trade when the most apparent opportunity comes next to you. You'll know you've arrived when you can shrug off poor opportunities with a shrug of the shoulder.

Take your time if you're new to all of this. Evaluate the two scenarios: After just one lesson, will you believe yourself capable of doing neurosurgery? Even though the concepts would be the same, the same is true in trading and even more so in options trading. Give yourself plenty of time to study. It is the next stage if you're already familiar with stocks.

And, just as you had to get used to trading stocks at first, you'll have to get used to trading options now. Furthermore, after you've gained enough confidence to trade, you'll need the patience to trade. Even if we weren't sure it was the wisest move, we've all did a poor job of investing too quickly. So, remain calm, take a deep breath if you need to, and keep to your trading approach at all times.

Lastly, perseverance requires employing an investment strategy that capitalizes on the passage of time while also safeguarding your capital. There are several options accessible to you, but you may always choose to keep things simple. Regardless matter which path you take, always be on the watch for the right opportunity.

When it comes to accumulating wealth, be patient. In this regard, the more patient you are, the better off you will be. Allow yourself time to learn, gain experience, and then put what you've learned into practice regularly so that you may start making money and accumulating wealth.

Perseverance

If you believe in something, you must persevere until you achieve your objective. Set a new objective once you've achieved your first one.

You must stick to your aim of becoming a successful trader, whether full-time or part-time, if you want to succeed. It's a simple task that anyone can complete. It has been witnessed in numerous learners' time and time again, where even the most unlikely characters, even those who don't think they can, can become outstanding traders. Is being realistic, set reachable goals that you can achieve in a reasonable amount of time. So, by next week, you'll know everything there is to know about the four basic risk profiles. It's possible that you'll be able to finish it tonight. Continue to establish reasonable goals but make them a little more challenging, and You'll be capable of keeping up the huge learning pace. As you develop, your confidence will grow as you prove to yourself that you can understand everything you set your mind for.

Knowledge

After you've established the importance of patience in both gathering information and trading, remember that knowledge may now be accessed with such ease and speed that it may be obtained in a reasonable length of time. These days there are now technologies that can be used to simulate the trading experience and a range of publications and websites to help you expand your knowledge collection. The best information comes from experience. "Trading programmatically," it's all well and well to say, but few people actually do. Because emotions are a natural component of our beings, it is preferable to work with them rather than disregard them. That's what my trading technique is all about: being secure but still having a chance to make a lot of money. Keep in mind; learning is a process that requires practice. Isn't it true that we can all recall the craziest of our professors from school? You can remember the funniest, scariest, smelliest, prettiest, and ugliest teachers. Still, it is guaranteed you can't recollect much about the professors who were in the middle, those who hardly made an experimental impact on you in years of being in the same classroom.

Similar may be said about trading. Trading necessitates a great deal of experience-based learning. In reality, hands-on experience is the most effective way to learn about trading. In both good and bad periods, it is through extraordinary experiences that you learn more about yourself. Most brilliant traders have had bad luck but, more importantly, have risen to the occasion and implemented what they've learned.

Honesty

If you want to turn out to be a good trader or investor, you must be honest with yourself. In the end, your performance is determined by your results. It is your duty, not anybody else's, to make decisions. It never helps to place blame on others. You are the one in power if you pull the trigger.

Pre-Planning

Every trade must be planned ahead of time. You must be aware of your surroundings in order to do so.

- Maximum risk
- Breakeven points
- Maximum reward

You must also arrange your

- Entrance
- Escape routes, whether it is to
- Make money or Eliminate losses

When the underlying stock usually determines trading options, your stop-loss. It's easier to make a loss-cutting choice based on the underlying stock's price, future, or whatever the underlying value is because of the underlying stock, future, or whatever the underlying asset is usually still more fluid than its options. The selection of the underlying asset is the first element of pre-planning due to the chart pattern. The trading strategy is then created, which demands.

Discipline—The Key to Success

It's critical not to waste the knowledge you've worked so hard to obtain and use the principles outlined previously. You must be self-disciplined and keep to that discipline consistently.

This implies that:

- You constantly plan ahead of time
- drawing on your (and others') expertise,
- sticking to your stated rational strategy.

This is the first step in becoming more methodical. Trading requires a high level of discipline. Even the most sophisticated trading systems will fail if money management is not in place. However, you can keep your losses to a minimum and your gains to increase by following basic cash principles.

CHAPTER 2

What are OPTIONS?

Options are one of the most popular trading vehicles because their prices can vary quickly, allowing traders to quickly make (or lose) a lot of money. Of course, options trading entails more significant risk than traditional stock market investing, but it's also more engaging and thrilling, with a significant potential upside.

The fantastic part for new investors is that they can begin earning with as little as a $100 investment. The call and the put are the two basic types of options that use in all options strategies.

Call Options

Call options are contracts that let investors the right to buy 100 shares of stock over a specified time period. Investors will purchase call options if they feel the value of a stock or security will rise. They can profit from the higher value of the shares when they sell them by purchasing these options at a predetermined price.

Put-Options

Put options are the particular opposite of call options; they allow investors to sell a specific number of shares over a specified period. Because of this difference, investors usually hope for a higher strike price in order to profit since this indicates a better value for the option. Essentially, you want the price of the security or shares to fall when you buy put options.

The Valuation of Options

The underlying assets from which options are derived are completely independent entities (hence, the term derivative). They do, however, have a worth in and of itself, which can be broken down into two types: intrinsic value and time value.

Generally speaking:

- Intrinsic value refers to the portion of an option's value that is in the money (ITM).
- The time value is the remainder of the option's value. Out-of-the-money options will have no inherent value

and will be evaluated only on temporal value. Hope value is another term for time value. This expectation is based on the remaining time till expiration and the underlying asset's price.

- When the price of the underlying asset exceeds the strike price, the call is in the money.
- When the asset's worth is less than the market price, the call is out of the money.
- A call is at-the-money (ATM) when the strike price and the underlying asset price are identical. The reverse is true with put options.
- When the price of the asset is less than the market price, the put is in the money.
- When the trader is greater than the market price, the put is out of the money.
- A put is "AT the market " when the market rate and the rate of the underlying asset are the same.

What Is Options Trading?

The process of purchasing and selling options on the market is known as options trading. This activity necessitates a thorough awareness of the market and the capacity to forecast price fluctuations.

Options are popular among investors because they require a lower initial commitment than buying equities outright. Because contracts are typically six months lengthy, buyers have time to watch their investments play out.

Looking at an options trading example is the most excellent approach for a beginner to grasp options trading.

Let's say you wish to purchase 100,000 shares of XYZ stock at $5 per share. But either you don't have the funds to purchase that much right now, or you're concerned that the price will drop. So, you pay $5,000 for the option to buy at $5 per share. You can now lawfully purchase XYZ stock for $5 per share, regardless of the share price; the contract is for a month.

Let's imagine XYZ Company reports better-than-expected earnings a few days later and claims to have devised a machine that would end world hunger. The stock rises from $5 to $50 per share in a single day. You exercise your option and spend $500,000 to purchase stock worth $5,000,000. You then sell it for a profit of $4,495,000 ($5 million - $500,000 - $5,000).

Let's pretend the situation is reversed. The XYZ Corporation declares bankruptcy and ceases to exist. The stock has dropped from \$5 to \$0. You can let your option lapse into nothingness, and you'll just lose \$5,000.

Options that are both deliverable and cash-settled

A deliverable settled option is one in which the underlying stocks or assets on which the option is based must be transferred.

Some option contracts are settled in cash. This means that the difference in the strike and expiry prices will be paid out in cash.

Why Use Options?

Options trading is used for speculating or hedging purposes. Hedge fund managers are known for hedging their market exposure with superior risk management procedures.

Options provide a lot of leverage, allowing you to trade large contracts and potentially make more money. This is also correct in the Forex market.

Buying stocks outright requires a larger initial commitment. When purchasing options, the risk is partial to the premium paid up front.

The risk is reduced by using options, but the potential profit is theoretically unlimited. Obviously, when we say theoretically endless earnings, we mean exactly that.

Benefits of Trading Options

Some of the reimbursements of trading options include:

- **It is cost-effective:** Options have huge leverage power, allowing investors to obtain an option position equivalent to stocks at a cheaper cost.
- **Less risky:** Options trading, when done correctly, can be less dangerous than stock ownership. This is because, in comparison to equities and related markets, options need a lower financial commitment.
- **Higher possible ROI:** When you trade options, you spend less money and make the same amount of money as when you trade stocks. The rate of return on options is higher than the rate of return on stocks.
- **Investors like synthetic position:** In options trading, synthetic positions give traders more options for achieving the same investing goals. Options trading also provides traders with a variety of strategy options.

CHAPTER 3

Option Trading Strategies for Beginners

A breakdown of their benefit and risk, as well as when a trader might use them. While these methods are simple, they have the potential to make a trader a lot of money – but they are not without danger. Here are some options trading strategies for beginners.

1. Buying Calls

When a trader buys a call – referred to as "going long" a call – with the expectation that the stock price will exceed the strike price by the expiration date. If the stock soars, the upside on this strategy is limitless, and traders can profit several times their initial investment.

It is the key strategy for traders who:

- Are you "bullish" or confident in a certain stock, ETF, or index and wish to keep risk to a minimum?
- Want to take advantage of rising prices by using leverage

Example 1:

Let's say a trader wishes to put $5,000 into Apple (AAPL), which is now trading at $165 per share. They can buy 30 shares for $4,950 with this sum. Assume that the stock price rises by 10% to $181.50 in the next month. The trader's portfolio will grow to $5,445 after any brokerage, commission, or transaction costs are deducted, for a net dollar return of $495, or 10% on the money invested.

Let's assume a call option on the stock with a $165 strike price expires in a month costs $5.50 per share or $550 per contract. The trader's available investment budget allows them to purchase nine options for $4,950. The trader is basically making a deal on 900 shares because the option contract controls 100 shares. The option will expire in cash and be worth $16.50 per share ($181.50-$165 strike), or $14,850 on 900 shares if the stock price rises 10% to $181.50 at expiry. When compared to trading the underlying asset directly, it equates to a net dollar return of $9,990, or a 200 percent return on investment.

Buying Call Graphical Representation:

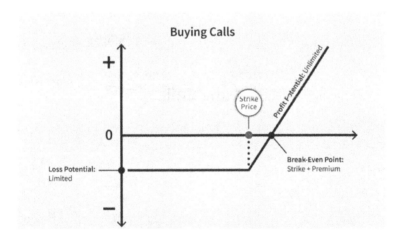

Example 2:

Stock X is currently trading at $20 per share, and a call with a $20 strike price plus a four-month expiration is trading at $1.

The contract costs $100, which is equal to one contract * $1 * 100 shares per contract.

Stock Price	Profit
$80	$2,500
$70	$1,500
$60	$500
$55	$0
$50	($500)
$40	($500)
$30	($500)
$20	($500)

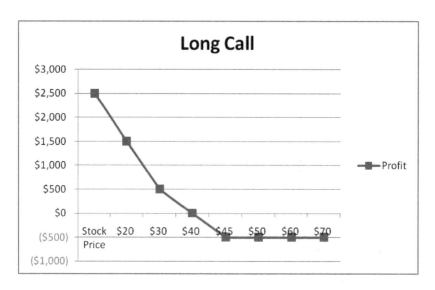

Risk/reward: As long as the stock climbs higher and the call is well-timed, the upside on a long call is potentially unlimited until expiration. Even if the stock falls in value, traders can frequently recover some of the premia by selling the call before it expires. The disadvantage is that the premium paid will be lost entirely.

As in Example 2, the trader breaks even at $21 per share, or the strike price plus the $1 premium paid. For every dollar the stock rises above $20, the option earns $100 in value. When the stock is at or below the strike price, the option expires worthless.

Why want to utilize it?

A long call is a strategy to bet on a stock rising and generate significant additional turnover than if you owned the stock directly if you don't mind losing the entire premium. It can also be a technique to reduce the risk of directly owning the stock.

2. Buying Puts

When the trader buys a put – referred to as "going long" a put – with the expectation that the stock price will be below the strike price by expiration, if the stock falls dramatically, the profit on this trade can be many twice the initial investment.

This is the recommended approach for traders who:

- Are negative on a specific stock, ETF, or index but don't want to take on as much risk as a short-selling strategy would.
- Want to use leverage to profit from dropping prices.

The long put is similar to the long call, except instead of betting on a stock's increase, you're betting for its decline. An investor purchases a put option, betting that the stock will fall below the strike price by the time it expires.

Buying Put Graphical Representation:

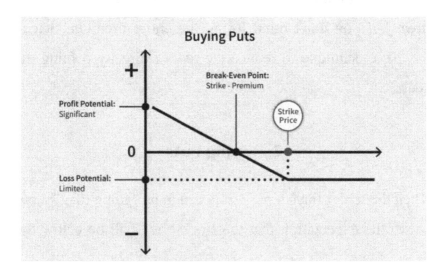

Example 1:

XYZ stock is currently trading at $50 per share, and a $50 strike put is available for $5 with a six-month expiration. The put costs $500 in total: the $5 premium multiplied by 100 shares. The payment profile of one long put contract is shown below.

Stock Price	Profit
$20	$2,500
$30	$1,500
$40	$500
$45	$0
$50	($500)
$60	($500)
$70	($500)
$80	($500)

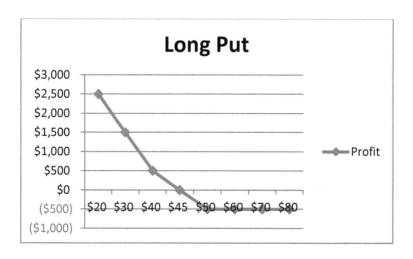

Example 2:

Stock X is currently trading at $20 per share, and a put with a $20 strike price and a four-month expiration is now trading at $1. The contract costs $100, which is equal to one contract * $1 * 100 shares per contract.

The profit on the long put at expiration is shown below.

Stock Price	Profit
$15	$400
$16	$300
$17	$200
$18	$100
$19	$0

$20	($100)
$21	($100)
$22	($100)
$23	($100)
$24	($100)
$25	($100)

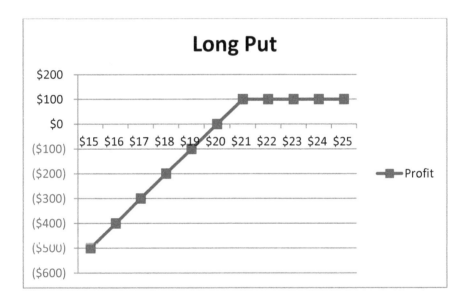

Risk/Reward:

The amount of money you could lose is restricted to the premium you paid for the options. Because the underlying price cannot go below zero, the maximum profit from the position is limited, but the put option, like a long call option, magnifies the trader's return.

Because the gain might be multiples of the option premium paid, the upside on a long put is virtually as good as it is on a long call. On the other hand, a stock can never go below zero, limiting its upward potential, but a long call has virtually unlimited potential. As a result, long puts are a popular and straightforward way to bet on a stock's decline, and they can be safer than shorting a stock.

A long put's downside is limited to the premium paid. If the stock ends above the strike price before the option expires, the put will be worthless, and you will lose your money.

In example 2, When the stock closes at $19 per share at option expiration, or the strike price minus the $1 premium paid, the put breaks even. For every dollar the stock falls below $19, the put rises in value by $100. The put expires worthless above $20, and the trader loses the entire $100 premium.

In the same way, $5,000 is $5,000 in Example 1. Even if the stock rises, traders can still sell the put and save some of the premia if there is enough time until the expiration date. The worst-case scenario is a complete loss of the premium or $500 in this case.

Why want to utilize it?

If you can tolerate the risk of losing the entire premium, a long put is a way to bet on a stock's downfall. Traders who own puts instead of shorting the stock will make substantially more money if the stock falls significantly. When compared to short-selling, where the risk is unbounded because a stock's price might theoretically continue growing indefinitely and has no expiration date, some traders may employ a long put to limit their potential losses.

3. Covered Call

A covered call is similar to selling a call option but with a twist. In this case, the trader sells a call while also purchasing 100 shares of the stock underlying the option. By owning the stock, you may turn a potentially risky investment - a short call – into a relatively safe and profitable one. At expiration, traders expect the stock price to be lower than the strike price. The owner should sell the stock to the call buyer at the strike price if the stock ends above the strike price.

This is a preferred position for traders who:

- Are you ready to limit upward potential in return for some downside protection

- Expect no change or a little increase in the underlying's price

Understanding Covered Calls

Covered calls are a neutral strategy, which means that the investor only expects a minor increase or reduction in the underlying stock price during the course of the written call option's life. This technique is frequently used when an investor has a short-term neutral outlook on an asset and, as a result, retains the asset long while also holding a short position via an option to profit from the option premiums. Simply put, if an investor plans to keep the underlying stock for a long time but does not expect a significant price increase in the near future, they can make income (premiums) for their account while waiting out the lull.

A covered call is a short-term hedge on a long stock position that allows investors to profit from the premium paid to write the option. However, if the price rises above the option's strike price, the investor loses his stock profits. If the buyer chooses to perform the option, they must provide 100 shares at the strike price for each contract made. A covered call strategy is ineffective for both bullish and bearish investors. If an investor is extremely bullish, it is usually preferable not to write the option and instead keep the stock. If the stock price surges, the option caps the profit on the stock, which could limit the overall profit of the investment.

Covered Call Graphical Representation:

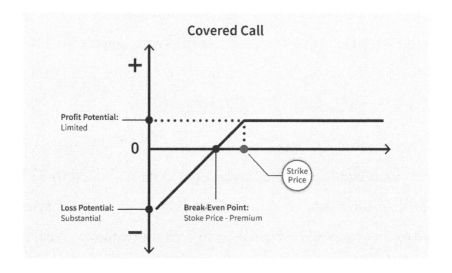

Example 1:

A hypothetical corporation, TSJ, is owned by an investor. They favor the company's long-term prospects and share price but believe the stock will trade relatively flat in the short term, perhaps within a couple of dollars of its present $25 price. Thus, they get the premium from the option sale but limit their upside on stock to $27 for the period of the option if they sell the call option on TSJ with a strike price of $27. Assume they get $0.75 for each contract ($75 per contract or 100 shares) for writing a three-month call option.

There will be one of two scenarios:

• TSJ stock is currently trading below the $27 strike price. Therefore, the option will expire worthlessly, and the investor will keep the premium. In this situation, they were able to outperform the stock by using the buy-write approach. They still hold the stock, but they now have an extra $75 in their pocket because of the reduced expenses.

• The price of TSJ stock has risen above $27. The option is exercised, and the stock's upward potential is limited to $27. The investor would be better off holding the stock if the price increases above $27.75 (strike price plus premium). Writing the call option gave them an extra $0.75 per share if they planned to sell at $27 anyway.

Example 2:

XYZ stock is currently trading at $50 a share, and a call with a strike price of $50 may be purchased for $5 with a six-month expiration. The call is sold for $500 in total, including the $5 premium multiplied by 100 shares. The bank invests or already owns 100 XYZ shares.

Stock Price	Call Profit	Stock Profit	Total Profit
$20	$500	($3,000)	($2,500)

$30	$500	($2,000)	($1,500)
$40	$500	($1,000)	($500)
$50	$500	$0	$0
$60	$500	$1,000	$500
$70	$0	$2,000	$500
$80	($500)	$3,000	$500
$90	($1,500)	$4,000	$500
$100	($2,500)	$5,000	$500

Covered Call

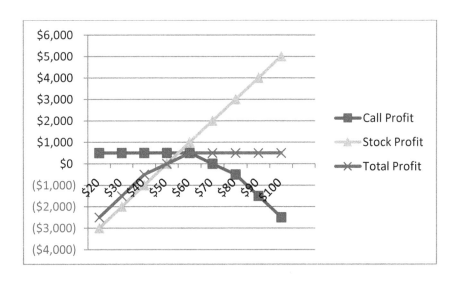

Example 3:

Stock X is currently trading at $20 per share, and a call with a
$20 strike price and a four-month expiration is now trading at

33

$1. The contract pays a $100 premium, which is equal to one contract * $1 * 100 shares per contract. For $2,000, the trader purchases 100 shares of stock and sells one call for $100.

Stock Price	Total Profit
$15	($500)
$16	($400)
$17	($300)
$18	($200)
$19	($100)
$20	$0
$21	$100
$22	$100
$23	$100
$24	$100
$25	$100

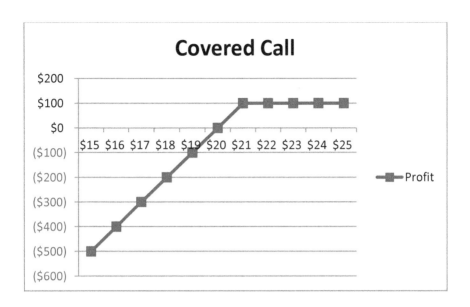

Covered Call

Reward/risk:

In Example 3, the trader makes a profit of $19 per share, which is the strike price less the $1 premium received. The trader would lose money if the price fell below $19, as the stock would lose money, more than compensating the $1 premium. The trader would keep the entire premium and the stock if the price were exactly $20. The gain is restricted at $100 once it reaches $20. Although the short call loses $100 for every dollar increase above $20, the stock's rise completely offsets the loss, leaving the trader with the original $100 premium as the total profit.

Nevertheless, of how high the stock price rises, the covered call's upside is restricted to the premium received. You won't be able to make plenty more, but you can lose a lot more. The short call entirely cancels out any gains you would have made if the stock had risen.

If the stock decreases, the downside is a complete loss of the stock investment, which is countered by the premium earned. If the stock falls, the covered call exposes you to a big loss. For example, if the stock fell to zero in our case, the total loss would be $1,900.

Similarly, if the stock remains at or just below the strike price at expiration, the covered call's maximum upside is the premium, or $500. The call option gets more expensive as the stock goes above the strike price, neutralizing most stock gains and limit upside. Call sellers may lose a stock profit that they would have made if they hadn't set up a covered call, but they don't lose any additional capital because the upside is capped. Meanwhile, the stock's potential downside is a total loss of $4,500, less the $500 premium.

Why should you utilize it?

The covered call is favored by investors searching for a low-risk way to produce income while expecting the stock to stay flat or slightly lower until the option expires.

Investors can also utilize a covered call to get a better sell price for a stock by selling calls at a higher strike price than they would be willing to sell the stock. In case if XYZ stock is trading at $50, an investor might sell a $60 strike call for $2, then:

• If the stock rises over the strike price before expiration, the call seller must sell the stock at the strike price, plus a bonus for the premium. The stock is worth a total of $62 per share to the investor, which includes the $60 strike price plus the $2 premium previously received.

• If the stock remains below the strike price at expiration, the call seller keeps the money and can repeat the strategy.

4. Married put

This approach is similar to the long put, but with a difference. The trader buys a put and owns the underlying stock. It is a hedging transaction in which the trader expects the stock to rise but needs "insurance" if it drops. If the stock does drop, the long put will compensate for the loss.

This is the favored position for traders who:

• Purchases put options for the same number of shares.

• At a higher strike price, sell the same number of call options.

How a Married Put Works

For investors, a married put operates similarly to an insurance policy. It's a bullish technique used when an investor is concerned about the stock's near-term risks. The investor retains the benefits of stock ownership, such as dividends and the opportunity to vote, by retaining the stock with a protective put option. Alternatively, while having a call option is equally optimistic as owning the stock, it does not provide the same rewards. Because the underlying stock's price appreciation has no bounds, both a married put and a long call have the same limitless profit potential. However, because the cost or premium of the put option acquired decreases earnings, profit is always lower than if the stock were merely held. The approach hits breakeven when the underlying stock rises by the amount of the options premium paid. Anything above that is profit.

The advantage of a married put is that the stock now has the floor beneath it, lowering its downside risk. The floor is the difference between the underlying stock's price at the time of the married put's purchase and the put's strike price. To put it another way, if the underlying stock traded exactly at the strike price when the option was purchased, the strategy's loss is capped at a price paid for the option.

Because it has the same profit profile as a synthetic long call, a married put is also stated to as a synthetic long call. The technique is similar to buying a standard call option (without the underlying stock) in that both have the same dynamic: limited loss, infinite profit potential. The only difference between both tactics is how much less money is needed to buy a long call.

Married Put Graphical Representation:

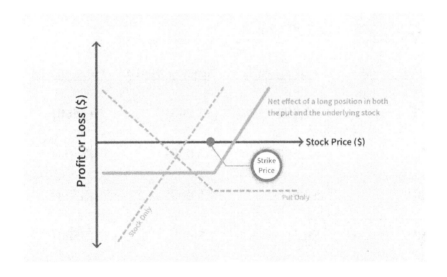

Example 1:

Let's say a trader purchases 100 shares of XYZ stock at $20 each and one XYZ $17.50 put for $0.50 (100 shares x $0.50 =

$50). They have purchased a stock position at the cost of $20 per share and a kind of insurance to protect themselves if the stock falls below $17.50 before the put's expiration date. The put and the stock must be purchased on the same day for a put to be termed "married," and the trader must notify their broker that the stock they just acquired will be carried if the put is exercised.

Example 2: XYZ stock is currently trading at $50 per share, and a $50 strike put is available for $5 with a six-month expiration. The put costs $500 in total: the $5 premium multiplied by 100 shares. XYZ is already owned by the investor, who has 100 shares.

Stock price	Put's profit	Stock's profit	Total profit
$20	$2,500	($3,000)	($500)
$30	$1,500	($2,000)	($500)
$40	$500	($1,000)	($500)
$50	$0	($500)	($500)
$60	($500)	$0	($500)
$70	($500)	$500	$0
$80	($500)	$1,000	$500

$90	($500)		$1,500
$100	($500)	$3,000	$2,500

Married Put

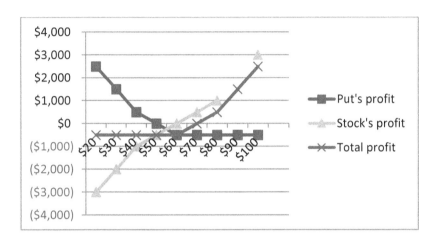

Example 3:

Stock X is currently trading at $20 per share, and a put with a $20 strike price and a four-month expiration is now trading at $1. The contract costs $100, which is equal to one contract * $1 * 100 shares per contract. Thus, the trader spends $2,000 on 100 shares of stock and $100 on a put.

Here's the profit on the married put strategy:

Stock Price	Total Profit
$15	($100)
$16	($100)

41

$17	($100)
$18	($100)
$19	($100)
$20	($100)
$21	$0
$22	$100
$23	$200
$24	$300
$25	$400

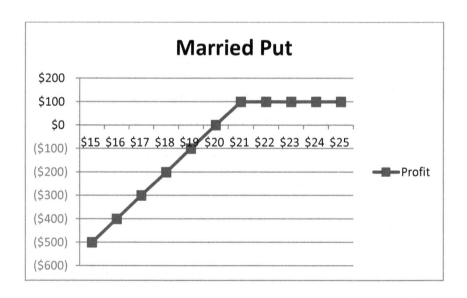

Reward/risk:

The married put in Example 3 breaks even at $21, which is the strike value plus the cost of the $1 premium. The long put compensates the stock's drop dollar for dollar below $20. Though the put expires useless and the trader loses the whole amount of the premium paid, $100 here, the total profit increases $100 for every dollar increase in the stock over $21.

As long as the stock continues to increase, less the cost of the put, the married put's maximum upside is theoretically limitless. Because the married put is in a hedged position, the premium represents the cost of ensuring the stock and allowing it to appreciate with limited downside risk.

The cost of the premium paid is the married put's disadvantage. As the value of the stock position declines, the put appreciates in value, dollar for dollar compensating the loss. Thus, the trader merely loses the cost of the option rather than the larger stock loss due to this hedge.

In Example 2, the upside is determined by whether the stock rises or falls. The maximum gain is potentially limitless, minus the premium of the long put, if the married put allowed the investor to keep owning a rising stock. If the stock drops, the put pays out, often matching any falls and offsetting the stock's loss minus the premium, capping the downside at $500. After the expiration date, the investor might continue to hold the stock for future profits.

When should you utilize it?

A married put is a capital preservation strategy rather than a profit-making approach. In fact, the cost of the strategy's put element becomes a built-in cost. Thus, if the underlying stock rises, the put price reduces the strategy's profitability by the cost of the option. As a result, investors should utilize a married put as a hedge against near-term uncertainty in an otherwise bullish stock or as a protection against a price breakdown.

New investors gain from the knowledge that their stock losses are restricted. As people learn more about various investing strategies, this might give them confidence. But, of course, this security comes at a price, which includes the option's cost, commissions, and maybe other costs.

5. Short Put

This strategy is the inverse of the long put, in which the trader sells a put, also known as "going short" a put, and expects the stock price to rise above the strike price by the expiration date. As a result, the trader earns a cash premium in exchange for selling a put, which is the highest a short put may earn.

This is the preferred strategy for traders who:

• When the stock closes below the strike price at option expiration, you want to buy it at the strike price

Working of short puts

When a trade is started by selling a put, it is called a short put. The writer (seller) gets compensated for this action by receiving a premium for writing an option. The option writer's profit is restricted to the premium obtained.

Buying an option and then selling it is not the same as starting an options trade to open a position by selling a put. The sell order is used to end a position and lock in a profit or loss in the latter. The sell (writing) opens the put position in the former.

When a trader buys a short put, they are betting that the underlying price will remain above the strike price of the written put. If the underlying prices stay above the put option's strike price, the option will expire worthlessly, and the writer will keep the premium. Conversely, the writer could lose money if the underlying price falls below the strike price.

Some traders use short puts to purchase the underlying securities. Assume you want to buy a stock for $25, but it's now trading at $27. If you sell a put option with a $25 strike price, you must buy the shares at that price if the price goes below $25, which you always planned to do.

The advantage is that you were paid for drafting the option. If you were given a $1 premium for writing the option, your purchase price was effectively cut to $24. If the underlying price does not fall below $25, you keep the $1 premium.

Example 1:

Assume an investor is positive on XYZ Corporation, a hypothetical stock now trading at $30 per share. Over the following few months, the investor predicts the stock will steadily grow above $40. The trader could simply buy shares, but 100 shares would cost $3,000 in the capital. Writing a put option makes cash right away, but it could also result in a loss in the future, as could buying shares.

For $5.50, the investor writes one put option with a strike price of $32.50 and a three-month expiration. As a result, the maximum profit is $550 ($5.50 x 100 shares). ($32.50 -

$5.50) x 100 shares = $2,700 maximum loss. If the underlying goes to $0 and the put writer still needs to buy the shares for $32.50, the maximum loss occurs. The premium received partially offsets the loss.

Short Put Graphical Representation

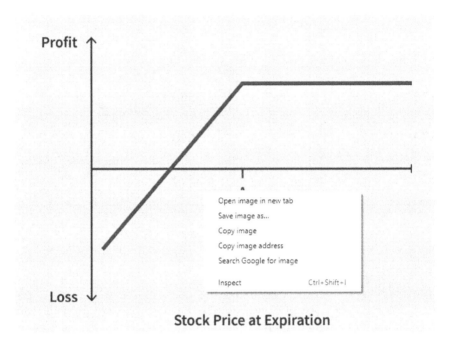

Stock Price at Expiration

Example 2:

XYZ stock is currently trading at $50 per share, and a $50 strike put may be purchased for $5 with a six-month expiration. The put is sold for $500 in total: the $5 premium multiplied by 100 shares. Thus, a short put's reward profile is the polar opposite of long puts.

Stock price	Short put's profit
$80	($2,500)
$70	($1,500)
$60	($500)
$50	$0
$45	$500
$40	$500
$30	$500
$20	$500

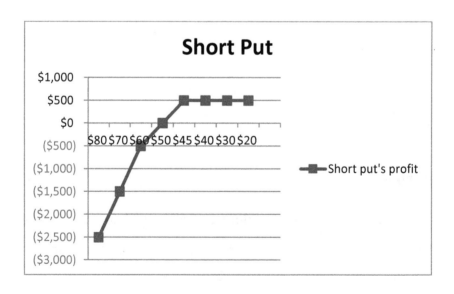

Example 3:

Stock X is currently trading at $20 per share, and a put with a $20 strike price and a four-month expiration is now trading at $1. The contract pays a $100 premium, which is equal to one contract * $1 * 100 shares per contract.

The profit on the short put at expiration is shown below.

Stock Price	Profit
$15	($400)
$16	($300)
$17	($200)
$18	($100)
$19	$0
$20	$100
$21	$100
$22	$100
$23	$100
$24	$100
$25	$100

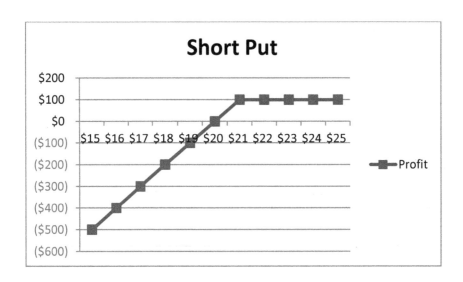

Reward/risk:

The short put in Example 3 breaks even at $19, or the strike price less the premium received. For every dollar of price reduction below $19, the short put loses the trader $100, while the put seller gains the whole $100 premium over $20. Between $19 and $20, the put seller would earn some, but not all, of the premium.

The short put's upside is always limited to the premium received, which in this case is $100. Like the short call or covered call, the maximum return on a short put is what the seller receives up front.

The whole value of the underlying stock less the premium received is the downside of a short put, and this is what would happen if the stock went to zero. In this case, the trader would have to buy $2,000 worth of stock (100 shares * $20 strike price), but the $100 premium received would negate this, resulting in a total loss of $1,900.

Like in Example 2, a long call bets on a significant increase in stock; a short put, on the other hand, is a more modest investment that pays out more modestly. The maximum return on a short put is the premium, or $500, which the seller receives upfront, but the long call can yield multiples of the original investment.

The seller keeps the entire premium if the stock stays at or rises above the strike price. If the stock continues below the strike price at expiration, the put seller is required to buy it at the strike price, resulting in a loss. If the price goes below $0 per share, the greatest downside happens. In that example, the short put would lose $5,000, or the strike price multiplied by 100 contracts.

Why should you utilize it?

Investors commonly use short puts to create income by selling the premium to other investors, speculating on a stock's decline. Put sellers, like insurance agents, want to sell the premium, so they don't have to pay it. However, investors should sell puts with caution, as they are obliged to buy shares if the stock falls below the strike price at expiration.

Any premiums earned from selling options can quickly be eaten away by a declining stock.

Investors sometimes use short puts to wager on a stock's appreciation because the deal needs no immediate cash investment. However, unlike a long call, the strategy's gain is limited, and it has a larger downside if the price falls.

Investors also use short puts to get a better purchasing price on an overpriced stock by selling options at a lower strike price than where they want to acquire the stock. For example, if XYZ stock is trading at $50, an investor might sell a $40 strike put for $2 and then:

- If the stock falls below the strike price at expiration, the put seller is allocated the equity, with the premium covering the purchase cost. Thus, the stock pays the investor a net $38 a share, which is the $40 strike price minus the $2 premium previously paid.
- If the stock stays above the strike price at expiration, the put seller keeps the money and can repeat the strategy.

6. Bull Call Spread

A bull call spread is an options trading technique that takes advantage of a stock's limited price gain. The method employs two call options to generate a strike price range with a lower and upper strike price. The bullish call spread aims to reduce stock losses while also limiting rewards.

Working of a bull call spread

The bull call spread is made up of the steps below, which include two call options.

- Pick an asset that you anticipate will appreciate slightly over a defined length of time (days, weeks, or months).
- Purchase and pay the premium for a call option with a strike price above the current market and a set expiration date.
- Collect the premium by simultaneously selling a call option with a higher strike price and the same expiration date as the first call option.

The premium received from selling the call option; partially compensates for the premium paid for the call by the investor.

In practice, investor debt is the cost of the strategy, which is the difference between the two call options.

The bull call spread lowers the call option's cost, but it comes with a cost. Gains in the stock's price are similarly limited, limiting the range in which the investor can profit. If traders feel an asset will rise in value moderately, they will use the bull call spread. They will most likely employ this method during periods of extreme volatility.

Because of the lower and upper strike prices, the bull call spread's losses and gains are limited. Therefore, the investor does not execute the option if the stock price falls below the lower strike price—the first acquired call option—at expiry.

The investor loses the net premium paid at the start of the option strategy because it expires worthless. They would have to pay more—the strike price—for an asset that is now selling less if they exercised the option.

If the stock price has climbed to the point that it is trading above the upper strike price—the second, sold call option— the investor executes their first option with the lower strike price. They can now buy the shares for a lower price than the current market value.

The second, sold call option, on the other hand, is still live. This call option will be automatically exercised or assigned by the options marketplace. The investor will sell the shares purchased with the lower strike option for the higher strike option.

As a result, the profit from buying the first call option is limited to the strike price of the sold option. The profit is equal to the difference between the lower and upper strike prices, minus the net cost or premium paid at the outset, of course. Thus, the risk associated with a bull call spread is reduced because the investor can only lose the net cost of creating the spread. The strategy's disadvantage is that the gains are restricted as well.

Bull Call Spread Graphical Representation

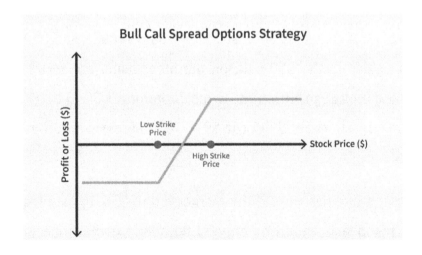

Example

When Citigroup (C) is trading at $49 per share, an options trader buys 1 Citigroup (C) June 21 call at the $50 strike price and pays $2 per contract.

Simultaneously, the trader sells one Citi June 21 call at the $60 strike price for $1 per contract. The trader's net cost to generate the spread is $1.00 per contract, or $100 because he paid $2 and received $1. ($2 long call premium minus $1 short call profit = $1 x 100 contract size = $100 net cost plus your broker's commission fee)

Both options expire worthless if the price falls below $50, and the trader loses the premium paid of $100 or the net cost of $1 per contract.

The value of a $50 call would rise to $10 if the prices jumped to $61, but the value of a $60 call would remain at $1. Any more gains in the $50 call, on the other hand, are forfeited, and the trader's profit on the two call options is $9 ($10 gain - $1 net cost). Thus, $900 (or $9 x 100 shares) would be the whole profit.

To put it another way, if the market fell to $30, the strategy's maximum loss would be only $1.00, while if the price went up to $100, the strategy's maximum gain would be $9.

Why should you utilize it?

Because the investor can only lose the net cost of creating the spread with a bull call spread, the losses are limited, lowering the risk. In addition, the net cost is also lower since the premium received from selling the call offsets the cost of the premium paid to buy the call.

Traders will utilize the bull call spread if they feel an asset's value will rise just enough to support activating the long call but not enough to justify executing the short call.

7. Bear Put Spread

A bear put spread is an options strategy in which an investor or trader expects a moderate-to-large decrease in a security or asset price and seeks to lower the cost of holding the option contract. A bear put spread is created by buying put options and selling the same amount of puts on the same asset at a lower strike price on the same expiration date. The maximum profit using this strategy is equal to the difference between the two strike prices minus the net cost of the options.

Working of a bear call spread

Consider the case of a stock that is now trading at $30. Buy one put option contract with a strike price of $35 for $475

($4.75 x 100 shares/contract) and sell one put option contract with a strike price of $30 for $175 ($1.75 x 100 shares/contract) to create a bear put spread.

In this situation, the investor will have to pay a total of $300 ($475 – $175) to set up this method. The investor will get a total profit of $200 if the underlying asset's price closes below $30 at expiration. This profit is calculated as $500 ($35 – $30) x 100 shares/contract – $300, and the net price of the two contracts [$475 – $175] = $200.

The key benefit of a bear put spread is that it lowers the overall risk of the deal. The cost of purchasing the put option with the higher strike price is covered by selling the put option with the lower strike price. As a result, the net capital outlay is lower than if you got a new put outright. It also bears significantly less risk than shorting a stock or investment because the risk is confined to the bear put spread's net cost. When selling a stock short, the risk is theoretically unlimited if the stock rises.

A bear put spread could be an excellent play if the trader feels the underlying stock or investment will decline by a specific amount between the trading date and the expiration date. If the underlying stock or investment falls by a larger amount, the trader forfeits the right to claim the additional profit.

Many traders are attracted to the trade-off between risk and potential return.

If the underlying share closes at $30, the lower strike price, at expiration, the profit from the bear put spread reaches its maximum. There will be no more profit if it closes below $30. There will be a decreased profit if it closes between the two strike prices. And if it closes over the higher strike price of $35, the entire money spent to buy the spread will be lost.

Option holders also do not influence when they are required to satisfy the obligation, as they do with any short position. Thus, early assignment, or the need to buy or sell the allocated number of the asset at the agreed-upon price, is always a possibility.

Bear Put Spread Graphical Representation

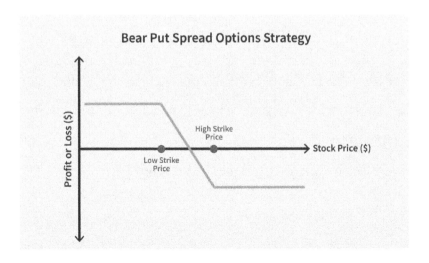

Example:

Let's say Levi Strauss & Co. (LEVI) is now trading at $50 on October 20, 2019. Winter is nearing, and you don't think the jeans company's stock will fare well. Instead, you believe it will be moderately depressing. So you buy a $40 put for $4 and a $30 put for $1. Both contracts were up for renewal on November 20, 2019. So, you would lose $3 ($4 − $1) if you purchased the $40 put and sold the $30 put at the same time.

Your maximum loss would be $3 if the stock finished over $40 on November 20. On paper, your maximum gain would be $7—$10 if it ended under or at $30, but you'd have to deduct $3 for the other trade and any broker commission fees. The trade's break-even price is $37, which is equal to the higher strike price minus the trade's net debt.

8. Protective Collar

A protective collar is a type of options strategy that can provide short-term downside protection while also allowing you to profit when the market rises. The technicalities of launching this hedging technique are covered here.

A protective collar consists of:

- A position in the underlying securities that is long.
- A stock put option purchased to protect against a stock's downside risk.
- A put option executed on the stock to fund the purchase of the put

Both the put and the call are normally out-of-the-money (OTM) options, and their expiration dates must be the same. The strike prices of the put and call options constitute a "collar" for the underlying stock that is determined by the combination of a long put and short call options.

The "protective" aspect of this technique comes from the fact that the put position protects the stock from falling below a certain level until the put expires.

Because the collar's primary goal is to protect against downside risk, the strike price of the call written should be greater than the strike price of the put purchased.

If a company is trading at $50, and call with a strike price of $52.50 might be written, and put with a strike price of $47.50 may be purchased. Because the stock can be called away if it moves over the strike price, the $52.50 call strike price serves as a cap on the stock's gains. Similarly, the $47.50 put strike price acts as a floor for the stock, providing downside protection below this level.

Graphical Representation of protective collar

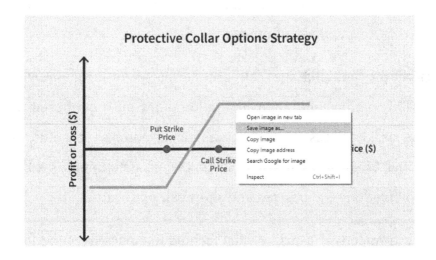

Working of the protective collar

A protective collar is typically used when an investor seeks short- to medium-term downside protection at a cheaper cost. Because buying protective puts can be costly, writing OTM calls can help offset the cost of the puts significantly.

In truth, most stocks can be protected using protective collars that are either "costless" (sometimes known as "zero-cost collars") or create a net credit for the investor.

The main disadvantage of this strategy is that the investor foregoes equity upside in exchange for downside protection.

The protective collar works wonders if the stock drops, but it fails miserably if the stock rises and is "called away," as any additional gain above the call strike price is lost. Thus, in the previous example, if a covered call is written at $52.50 on stock selling at $50, if the stock rises to $55, the investor who wrote the call must surrender the stock at $52.50, preceding a further $2.50 profit.

When the overall markets or single stocks are showing signs of reversing after a significant surge, protective collars are very effective. However, in a strong bull market, they should be utilized with care, as the chances of stocks being called away and therefore limit the upside of a given stock or portfolio are significant.

Example:

If an investor holds 100 shares of IBM at $50 and the stock increases to $100 on January 1, it is an example of this technique. By selling one IBM March 105 call and simultaneously buying one IBM March 95 put, the investor might create a protective collar. Until the expiration date, the trader is protected below $95 in value. Of course, the trade-off is that if IBM trades at $105 before expiration, they may be compelled to sell their shares at that price.

Constructing a Protective Collar

Let's look at how a protective collar might be built using a historical example from Apple, Inc. (AAPL) options, which closed at $177.09 on Jan. 12, 2018. 1 Assume you own 100 shares of Apple, which you purchased for $90. With the stock up 97 percent from its purchase price, you'd like to use a collar to secure your profits without selling them outright.

To begin, you must write a covered call on your Apple investment. Assume the March 2018 $185 calls are selling at $3.65 / $3.75, and you write one contract (with 100 AAPL shares as the underlying asset) to earn $365 in premium income (fewer commissions). You also spend $450 on one contract of March 2018 $170 puts, which are currently trading at $4.35 / $4.50. (plus commissions). The collar has a net cost of $85, excluding commissions.

9. Long Straddle

A long straddle is an options strategy in which the trader buys both a long call and a long put on the same underlying asset with the same expiration date and striking price on the same underlying asset.

How Long Straddle Works

The long straddle options strategy bets on the underlying asset's price moving significantly higher or lower. Regardless of which way the asset swings, the profit profile remains the same. Typically, the trader believes that the underlying asset will go from a low to a high volatility state due to the impending release of new data.

At-the-money or as close to it as possible is the strike price. Because calls profit from an upward advance in the underlying security and put benefit from a downward move, both of these components cancel out tiny moves in either direction. As a result, the purpose of a long straddle is to profit on a very significant rise in either direction by the underlying asset, which is frequently initiated by a newsworthy event.

A long straddle can be used by traders ahead of the news event, such as earnings report, Fed action, the passing of a law, or the election outcome. They believe the market is anticipating such an event; hence the trading is irregular and limited.

When the event occurs, all of the previously held bullish or bearish sentiment is released, causing the underlying asset to move swiftly. Of course, because the outcome of the actual event is unclear, the trader is unsure whether to be bullish or bearish. As a result, a long straddle is a sensible strategy for profiting from both scenarios. A lengthy straddle, like any other investment strategy, has its drawbacks.

The long straddle strategy carries the risk that the market may not respond strongly enough to the event or news it generates. This is exacerbated by the fact that option sellers are aware that the event is approaching, so they raise the prices of put and call options in anticipation of it.

This indicates that attempting the technique is far more expensive than betting on one direction alone and more expensive than betting on both directions if there is no newsworthy event.

Because option sellers realize that a scheduled, news-making event carries a higher risk, they raise prices to cover roughly 70% of the expected event. Because the straddle price already includes little swings in either direction, traders will find it much more difficult to profit from the move.

If the predicted event does not result in a significant move in either direction for the underlying securities, the trader's options will most likely expire worthless, resulting in a loss.

Long Straddle Construction

Long straddle positions have an unlimited profit potential while posing a low risk. The potential advantage is limitless if the price of the underlying asset continues to rise. Conversely, if the underlying asset's price falls to zero, the profit equals the strike price less the option premiums paid.

The total cost to enter the position, which is the price of the call option plus the price of the put option, represents the maximum risk in either instance.

The profit when the price of the underlying asset is increasing is given by

- Profit (up) = price of the underlying asset - the strike price of the call option - net premium paid
- The profit when the price of the underlying asset is decreasing is given by:
- Profit (down) = strike price of a put option - the price of the underlying asset - net premium paid

The total net premium paid, plus any trade commissions, are the maximum loss. At expiration, the underlying asset price equals the strike price of the options, resulting in a loss.

Graphical Representation of Long straddle

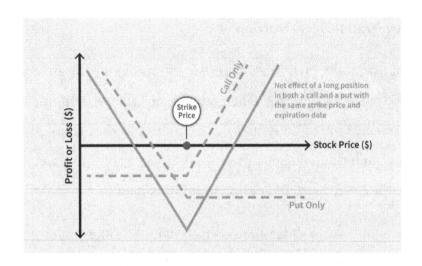

Notice how there are two breakeven points in the P&L graph above. When the stock makes a huge move in one direction or the other, this method becomes beneficial. The investor doesn't care which way the stock swings; all he cares about is that it moves more than the whole premium he paid for the structure.

Example:

The price of a stock is $50 per share. A call option with a $50 strike price costs $3, whereas a put option with the same strike costs $3. A straddle is formed when an investor buys one of each option.

This means that the option sellers believe there is a 70% chance that the stock will move $6 or less in either direction. Regardless of how the stock was initially priced, the position will benefit at expiration if it is valued above $56 or below $44.

Only if the stock is valued exactly at $50 after the expiration day does the maximum loss of $6 per share ($600 for one call and one put contract) occur. If the stock price is between $56 and $44 a share, the trader will experience a smaller loss.

If the stock is higher than $56 or lower than $44, the trader will profit. The position profit is (Profit = $65 - $50 - $6 = $9) if the stock moves to $65 at expiration.

Why should you utilize it?

Many traders believe that harnessing the expected spike in implied volatility is another way to use the long straddle. They would do so by launching this plan in the weeks running up to the event, say three weeks or more, then closing it (if profitable) immediately before the event. This approach tries to profit from rising option demand, which raises the implied volatility component of the options.

Increased implied volatility increases the price of all options puts and calls at all strike prices because implied volatility is the most powerful variable in the price of an option over time.

The directional risk is removed from the method by owning both the put and the call, leaving only the implied volatility component. As a result, if the trade is entered before implied volatility rises and exited when implied volatility reaches its high, the trade should be profitable.

The inherent tendency for options to lose value due to time decay is, of course, a shortcoming of this second strategy. To avoid this natural price drop, choose options with expiration dates that are unlikely to be greatly affected by time decay, also known as theta to option traders.

10. Long Strangle

A strangle is an options strategy in which the investor buys a call and a put option with separate strike prices but the same expiration date and underlying asset. If you believe the underlying asset will undergo a major price fluctuation in the near future but are unsure of the direction, a strangle is a suitable strategy to use. However, it is only profitable if the asset's price swings dramatically.

Working of Long strangle

They are two types of strangling:

- **Long strangle:** A long strangle a strategy in which an investor buys both an out-of-the-money call and an out-of-the-money put option at the same time. The call option's strike price is greater than the current market price of the underlying asset, while the strike price of the put option is lower. Because the call option has theoretically unlimited upside if the underlying asset grows in price, and the put option can benefit if the underlying asset falls in price, this approach has high-profit potential. The trade's risk is limited to the difference between the two options' prices.

- **Short strangle:** A short strangle is when an investor sells both an out-of-the-money put and an out-of-the-money call at the same time. This is a profit-limited strategy with a neutral attitude. When the price of the underlying stock trades in a small range between the breakeven points, a short strangle makes money.

Strangle vs. Straddle

Strangles and straddles are two options techniques that allow investors to profit from big upward or downward price movements. On the other hand, a long straddle entails simultaneously buying at-the-money call and put options rather than out-of-the-money options, where the strike price is similar to the underlying asset's market price.

A short straddle is similar to a short strangle in that it has a limited profit potential equal to the premium earned by selling at-the-money call and put options.

The investor earns from the straddle when the security price rises or decreases by an amount more than the entire cost of the premium from the strike price. As a result, there isn't as much of a pricing difference. As a result, buying a strangle is less expensive than purchasing a straddle, but it entails more risk because the underlying asset must make a larger move to achieve a profit.

Graphical Representation

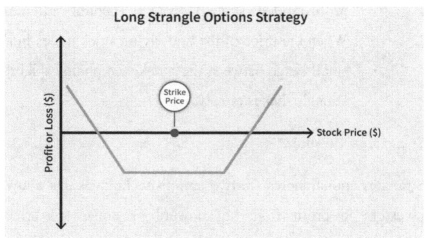

Notice how there are two breakeven points in the P&L graph above. When the stock makes a huge move in one direction or the other, this method becomes beneficial. The investor doesn't care which way the stock moves; all that matters is that it moves more than the whole premium paid for the arrangement.

Example 1:

Consider the case of Starbucks (SBUX), which is now trading at $50 per share. A trader uses the strangle option technique by taking two long option positions, one call and one put. The call has a $52 strike price and a $3 premium, totaling $300 ($3 x 100 shares). The put option's strike price is $48, and the premium is $2.85, totaling $285 ($2.85 x 100 shares). The expiration dates for both alternatives are the same.

If the stock price maintains between $48 and $52 for the option's duration, the trader will lose $585, which is equal to the total cost of the two option contracts ($300 + $285).

Let's imagine, on the other hand, Starbucks' stock is volatile. If the stock price reaches $38, the call option will expire worthlessly, and the $300 premium paid for it will be forfeited. On the other hand, the put option has increased in value, expiring at $1,000 and creating a net profit of $715

($1,000 less the initial option cost of $285). As a result, the trader has made a total profit of $415 ($715 profit - $300 loss).

The put option expires worthless if the price climbs to $57 and the $285 premium paid for is lost. The call option generates a $200 profit ($500 value less $300 cost). When the loss from the put option is taken into account, the trade loses $85 ($200 profit - $285) since the price change was insufficient to cover the cost of the options.

The key principle is that the move must be large enough. For example, if Starbucks' stock had increased $12 to $62 per share, the total gain would have been $415 ($1000 value – $300 call option premium minus $285 for an expired put option).

Example 2:

This strategy could be based on information from a company's earnings release or an event involving a Food and Drug Administration (FDA) approval for a pharmaceutical stock. Losses are restricted to the cost of both choices (the premium paid). Because the options purchased are out-of-the-money options, strangles are usually always less expensive than straddles.

11. Butterfly Spread

A butterfly spread is a type of option strategy that combines bull and bear spreads with defined risk and profit cap. These spreads, which can include four calls, four puts, or a combination of the two, are designed to be a market-neutral strategy that pays off the most if the underlying does not move before the option expiration date.

Working of butterfly spread

Four option contracts with the same expiration date but three different strike prices are used in butterfly spreads. A higher strike price, an at-the-money strike price, and a lower strike price are all examples of strike prices. The at-the-money options are the same distance away as the options with higher and lower strike prices. If the strike price of the at-the-money options is $60, the strike prices of the upper and lower options should be equal dollar amounts above and below $60. For example, at $55 and $65, these strikes are each $5 away from $60.

A butterfly spread can be made with puts or calls. Different forms of butterfly spreads can be created by combining the options in various ways, each designed to profit from either high or low volatility.

Long Call Butterfly Spread

Buying one in-the-money call option with a low strike price, writing two at-the-money call options, and buying one out-of-the-money call option with a higher strike price creates the long butterfly call spread. When you enter a trade, you create net debt.

If the underlying price at expiration is the same as the written calls, the maximum profit is attained. The maximum profit is determined by subtracting the strike of the written option from the strike of the lower call, premiums, and commissions paid. Thus, the maximum loss is equal to the amount paid in premiums plus commissions.

Short Call Butterfly Spread

Selling one in-the-money call option with a lower strike price, buying two at-the-money call options, and selling one out-of-the-money call option with a higher strike price makes up the short butterfly spread. When you take the job, you get a net credit. If the underlying price is above or below the upper strike or below the lower strike at expiry, this position maximizes profit.

The maximum profit is equal to the first premium received minus commission costs. Conversely, the maximum loss is equal to the bought call's strike price minus the lower strike price minus the premiums obtained.

Long Put Butterfly Spread

Buying one put with a lower strike price, selling two at-the-money puts, and buying a put with a higher strike price creates the long-put butterfly spread. When you take a position, you create net debt. Like the long call butterfly, this position makes the most money when the underlying stays at the strike price of the middle options.

The higher strike price minus the strike of the sold put, less the premium paid, equals the maximum profit. Thus, the trade's maximum loss is restricted to the premiums and commissions paid at the start.

Short Put Butterfly Spread

Writing one out-of-the-money put option with a low strike price, buying two at-the-money puts, and writing one in-the-money put option with a higher strike price results in the short put butterfly spread. If the underlying price is above the upper strike or below the lower strike price at expiration, this method makes the most money.

The premiums received are the strategy's maximum profit. The higher strike price minus the strike of the bought put, less the premiums collected, equals the maximum loss.

Iron Butterfly Spread

Buying an out-of-the-money put option with a lower strike price, writing an at-the-money put option, writing an at-the-money call option, and buying an out-of-the-money call option with a higher strike price makes up the iron butterfly spread. As a result, you'll have a transaction with a net credit that's excellent for low-volatility conditions.

The premiums are received to provide the most profit. Thus, the maximum loss is equal to the difference between the strike prices of the bought and written calls, less the premiums earned.

Reverse Iron Butterfly Spread

Writing an out-of-the-money put at a lower strike price, buying an at-the-money put, buying an at-the-money call, and writing an out-of-the-money call at a higher strike price from the reverse iron butterfly spread.

This results in a net debit trade that works best in high-volatility situations. When the price of the underlying moves above or below the higher or lower strike prices, the maximum profit is realized. The risk associated with the technique is limited to the premium paid to obtain the position. Thus, the maximum profit is equal to the difference between the strike prices of the written and bought calls, less the premiums paid.

Graphical Representation

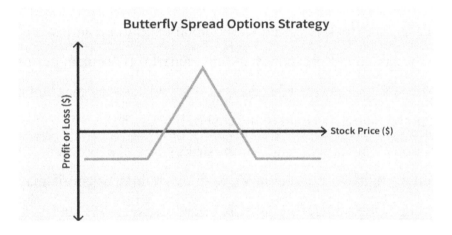

Notice how the biggest profit is made when the stock remains unchanged until expiration–at the moment of the at-the-money (ATM) strike–in the P&L graph above. The bigger the negative shift in the P&L as the stock travels away from the ATM strikes. When the stock closes at a lower strike or below, the maximum loss happens (or if the stock settles or above the higher strike call). This technique has limited upside potential as well as a restricted downside potential.

Example 1:

An investor predicts that Verizon stock, which is now priced at $60, will not move much in the next months. So, they decide to use a long call butterfly spread in order to benefit if the price stays the same.

An investor buys two extra calls at $55 and $65 and writes two call options on Verizon with a strike price of $60.

If Verizon stock is priced at $60 upon expiration, an investor will make the most money in this scenario. If Verizon closes below $55 or above $65, the investor will lose the maximum amount, which is equal to the cost of buying the two wing call options (the higher and lower strike) less the proceeds of selling the two middle strike options. A loss or profit may occur if the underlying asset is priced between $55 and $65. The amount of premium paid to be considered for the job is crucial. Assume that it costs $2.50 to apply for the job. As a result, if Verizon is priced at less than $60 minus $2.50, the position will lose money.

If the underlying asset were priced at $60 plus $2.50 at expiration, the result would be the same. The position would profit in this scenario if the underlying asset were priced between $57.50 and $62.50 at expiration.

Example 2:

Buy one in-the-money call option at a lower strike price, sell two at-the-money call options, and buy one out-of-the-money call option to create a long butterfly spread. The wing widths of a balanced butterfly spread will be the same. A "call fly" is a type of example that results in a net debit. When an investor believes the stock will not move much before expiration, they will buy a long butterfly call spread.

Characteristics of a Butterfly Spread

Four option contracts with the same expiration date but three different strike prices are used in butterfly spreads. A higher strike price, an at-the-money strike price, and a lower strike price are all examples of strike prices. The at-the-money options are the same distance away as the options with higher and lower strike prices. There is a maximum profit and a maximum loss for each type of butterfly.

Long Call Butterfly Spread Constructed

The long call butterfly spread is produced by buying one low-strike in-the-money call option, writing (selling) two at-the-money call options, and purchasing one higher-strike out-of-the-money call option. When you enter a trade, you create net debt.

If the underlying price at expiration is the same as the written calls, the maximum profit is achieved. The maximum profit is determined by subtracting the strike of the written option from the strike of the lower call, premiums, and commissions paid. Thus, the maximum loss is equal to the amount paid in premiums plus commissions.

Long Put Butterfly Spread Constructed

Buying one out-of-the-money put option with a low strike price, selling (writing) two at-the-money put options, and buying one in-the-money put option with a higher strike price creates the long-put butterfly spread. When you take a position, you create net debt. Like the long call butterfly, this position makes the most money when the underlying stays at the strike price of the middle options.

12. Iron Condor

An iron condor is a four-strike options strategy that consists of two puts (one long and one short) and two calls (one long and one short) with the same expiration date. When the underlying asset closes between the intermediate strike prices at expiration, the iron condor makes the most money. In other words, the idea is to profit from the underlying asset's low volatility.

The iron condor has a similar reward as a standard condor spread, but instead of using only calls or only puts, it utilizes both calls and puts. Thus, the condor and the iron condor are extensions of the butterfly spread and the iron butterfly.

Working of an iron condor

The iron condor approach offers minimal upside and downside risk because the high and low strike options or wings protect against big swings in either direction. Its profit potential is likewise constrained as a result of the reduced risk. The trader's optimum outcome for this technique is for all options to expire worthlessly, which is only achievable if the underlying asset closes at expiry between the middle two strike prices. If the trade is successful, there will very certainly be a cost to close it. However, even if it fails, the loss will be minimal.

The construction of the strategy is as follows:

1. Purchase an out-of-the-money (OTM) put with a strike price lower than the underlying asset's current price. This OTM put option will protect you from a big drop in the underlying asset's price.

2. Sell one (OTM) or at-the-money (ATM), put a strike price closer to the underlying asset's current price.

3. Sell one OTM or ATM call with a strike price higher than the underlying asset's current price.

4. Purchase one OTM call with a strike price higher than the underlying asset's current price. This out-of-the-money call option will protect you from a significant upward move.

The wings, which are further OTM alternatives, are both long positions. Because these options are further OTM, their premiums are smaller than the two written options, resulting in a net credit to the account when the trade is made.

It is possible to make the strategy lean bullish or bearish by picking alternative strike prices. If both middle strike prices are above the underlying asset's current price, for example, the trader anticipates a minor price increase by expiration. In any case, the trade has small profit potential and small risk.

Graphical Representation

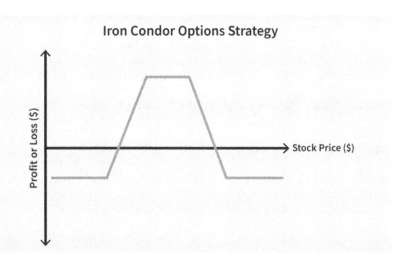

Notice how the biggest profit is made when the stock continues in a very wide trading range in the P&L graph above. As a result, the investor may be able to profit from the entire net credit earned when constructing the deal. The larger the loss up to the maximum loss, the further away the stock travels through the short strikes–lower for the put and higher for the call. The maximum loss is almost always greater than the maximum gain. This makes obvious sense, given that the structure has a larger chance of finishing with a minor benefit.

Iron Condor Profits and Losses

The amount of premium, or credit, received for generating the four-leg options position is the maximum profit for an iron condor.

There is also a limit to the amount of money you can lose. The difference between the long call and short call strikes, or the long put and short put strikes, is the maximum loss. To calculate the overall loss for the trade, subtract the net credits obtained from the loss and then add commissions.

If the price rises above the long call strike, which is higher than the sold call strike, or below the long-put strike, which is lower than the sold put strike, the maximum loss occurs.

Example:

Assume that an investor feels the price of Apple Inc. will remain relatively flat over the next two months. With the stock currently trading at $212.26, they decide to implement an iron condor. They sell a call with a strike price of $215 for $7.63 in premium and buy a call with a strike price of $220 for $5.35. Each options contract, put or call, amounts to 100 shares of the underlying asset; thus, the credit on these two legs is $2.28, or $228 for one contract. However, the deal is just half-finished.

In addition, the trader sells a put with a strike of $210 for $7.20 in premium and buys a put with a strike of $205 for $5.52 in premium. The net credit on these two legs is $1.68, or $168 if each leg is traded as a single contract.

The position's total credit is $3.96 ($2.28 + $1.68), or $396. This is the highest profit a trader may make if all of the options expire worthless, which means the price must be between $215 and $210 two months before expiration. The trader may still make a profit if the price is above $215 or below $210, but he or she may also lose money.

If Apple's stock price approaches the upper call strike ($220) or the lower put strike ($205), the loss will be greater. If the stock price trades above $220 or below $205, the maximum loss happens.

Assume the stock is worth $225 at the time of expiration. This is higher than the upper call strike price, implying that the trader is risking the most. The bought call makes $5 ($225 - $220), while the sold call loses $10 ($225 - $215). The puts are about to expire.

The trader loses $5 for a total loss of $500 (100 share contracts) but earns $396 in premiums. As a result, the total loss is limited to $104 plus commissions.

Assume that Apple's price fell instead, but not below the lower put level. The price drops to $208. The short put is worthless ($208 - $210), while the long put is useless ($208 - $210). The calls also have a time limit. The trader loses $200 on the position but received $396 in premium credits. As a result, excluding commission fees, they still make $196.

13. Iron Butterfly

An iron butterfly is a technique that uses four distinct contracts to profit from stocks or futures prices moving inside a set range. In addition, the trade is set up to profit from a drop in implied volatility. The key to making this transaction work as part of a profitable trading strategy is to predict when option prices are likely to fall in value. This frequently happens when the market is in a sideways or mildly upward trend. "Iron Fly" is another term for the trade.

Working of Iron Butterfly

The Iron Butterfly trade is made up of four options: two call options and two put options. There are three strike prices for these calls and puts, all with the same expiration date. The idea is to profit from scenarios where the price is relatively stable, and the implied and historical volatility of the options is dropping.

It's also possible to think of it as a combination option trade with a short straddle and a long strangle, with the straddle on the middle of the three strike prices and the strangle on two additional strikes above and below the middle strike price.

When the underlying asset closes exactly on the middle strike price at expiration, the trade makes the most money. For example, the steps below will help a trader build an Iron Butterfly trade.

1. The trader determines the price at which the underlying asset is expected to trade on a specific day in the future. This is the price that has been set as the target.

2. The trader will use options that expire on or near the day the target price is expected to be reached.

3. The financial plan one call option with a strike price that is significantly higher than the target price. At the time of expiration, this call option is predicted to be out-of-the-money. However, it will guard against a big increase in the underlying asset's price and limit any potential loss to a specified amount if the trade does not go as planned.

4. Using the striking price closest to the target price, the trader sells both a call and a put option. The strike price of this option will be lower than the call option

purchased in the previous stage and higher than the put option purchased in the next step.

5. The trader purchases one put option with a strike price that is significantly lower than the target price. At the time of expiration, this put option is predicted to be out-of-the-money. However, it will guard against a substantial drop in the underlying asset and limit any potential loss to a specified amount if the trade does not go as planned.

The option contracts offered in stages two and three should have strike prices that are far enough apart to account for a range of change in the underlying. As a result, rather than a small range near the target price, the trader will be able to forecast a range of successful price movements.

For example:

Suppose the trader believes that the underlying will trade at $50 in the next two weeks and will be within a five-dollar range of that price. In that case, the trader should sell a call and a put option with a strike price of $50 and buy a call option at least five dollars higher and a put option at least five dollars lower than the $50 target price.

In theory, this increases the chances that the price action will land and stay in a profitable range on or near the options' expiration date.

The Iron Butterfly's Deconstruction

By design, the strategy's upward profit potential is limited. It's a credit-spread method, which means the trader sells option premiums in exchange for a credit for the options' value at the start of the trade. The trader believes that the option's value will decline, resulting in a much lower value or no value at all. As a result, the trader hopes to keep as much credit as possible.

The approach has defined risk because the high and low strike options, or wings, guard against substantial moves in either direction. Because there are four possibilities involved in this technique, commission charges are always a consideration.

Traders will want to ensure that their broker's commissions do not significantly reduce their greatest potential earnings.

If the price stays inside a range near the center strike price as expiration day approaches, the Iron butterfly trade pays out. A short strangles center strike is the price at which the trader sells both a call and a put option.

As the price moves away from the center strike, either higher or lower, the transaction loses value and hits a maximum loss point as the price goes below the lower strike price or above, the higher strike price.

Graphically Presentation:

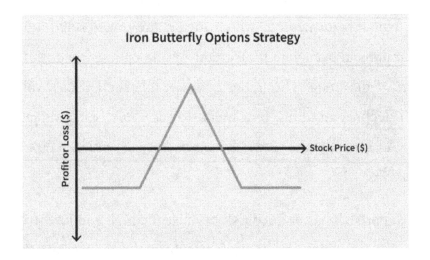

The largest profit is made when the stock remains at-the-money strikes of both the call and put that is sold, as shown in the P&L graph above. The total net premium received is the maximum gain. When the stock rises above the long call strike or below the long-put strike, the maximum loss occurs.

Example:

At IBM, the following chart demonstrates a trade setup using an Iron Butterfly.

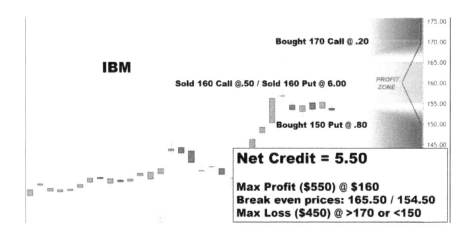

IBM

Bought 170 Call @ .20

Sold 160 Call @.50 / Sold 160 Put @ 6.00

PROFIT ZONE

Bought 150 Put @ .80

Net Credit = 5.50

Max Profit ($550) @ $160
Break even prices: 165.50 / 154.50
Max Loss ($450) @ >170 or <150

In this case, the trader forecasts a slight increase in the price of IBM shares over the next two weeks. This is because the company's earnings report was released two weeks ago, and the results were positive. Therefore, in the next two weeks, the trader predicts that the implied volatility of the options will generally decrease and that the stock price will rise. As a result, the trader initiates the transaction by taking in a net credit of $550 ($5.50 per share). So long as the price of IBM shares stays between 154.50 and 165.50, the trader will earn.

If the price remains below 160 on the day of expiration, the trader will have an additional trading chance. The trader can then let the trade expire and have the IBM shares (100 each put contract sold) delivered to them for $160 per share.

If the price of IBM closes at $158 per share on that day, and the trader lets the options expire, the trader will be required to purchase the shares for $160. All of the other option contracts expire worthlessly, so the trader doesn't have to do anything. This may appear as if the trader merely purchased shares for two dollars more than was required, but keep in mind that the dealer received an initial credit of $5.50 per share. As a result, the net transaction can be viewed in a different light. The trader purchased IBM shares while still making a $2.50 profit ($5.50 minus $2.00).

The majority of the Iron Butterfly trade impacts can be achieved in transactions with fewer options legs, resulting in lower commissions. Selling a naked put or buying a put-calendar spread are two options, but the Iron Butterfly provides low-cost protection from sharp downward moves that the naked put does not. The trade also benefits from falling implied volatility, which the put calendar spread is unable to achieve.

CHAPTER 4

How to Start OPTION Trading & Online Brokers?

You may be wondering how to get started now that you've learned about some of the options trading tactics accessible. The following stages should give you a good idea of how you can start using your options trading knowledge:

1. Know the requirements and create an account
2. Pick a Type of Option
3. Make Stock Price Predictions
4. Establish the Expiration Date

Know the requirements and create an account

Try to identify a strategy that appeals to you as you learn more about the many sorts of options trading. Take the time to write out your investment objectives, such as the amount of income you want to create, the amount of capital you have to invest, and the amount of portfolio growth you want to see. Begin looking for a broker to work with once you have a clearer idea of your financial objectives. They'll evaluate your financial readiness and assist you in opening a bank account.

Pick a Type of Option

Investigate various equities to choose which form of investment you wish to make, either a put or call option. Remember that if you expect stock prices to climb, you should buy a call option. If you predict them to fall, on the other hand, consider buying a put option. This phase is critical to the overall success of your investment, so do your homework on the assets you're considering.

Make Stock Price Predictions

Only if the contracts remain "in the money" can investors earn from options trading. This means that the share price must increase above the strike price for call options, but for put options, the share price must fall below the strike price. You must understand how to predict future changes in stock values and act accordingly; if you want to be successful while trading options. It's easier said than done, but with the correct study, you'll be astonished at how many forecasts you can make.

Establish the Expiration Date

The final decision that investors must make before acquiring options is the contract's expiration date. You risk losing money if you believe stocks will rise in value but are unsure if it will happen before your contract expires. The key to options trading is anticipating how stock prices will fluctuate and how they will change over time. Contracts can last from a few days to several years, with short-term contracts offering greater dangers than long-term contracts. Keep this in mind when you try to find expiration dates that are acceptable to you.

Best online options brokers for Trading

You should choose an online broker that allows you to trade options because not all do. You'll also want to ensure that any online broker you're contemplating is properly licensed in their home country and accepts clients from your country. Here are some best online options for brokers trading for beginners.

Tastywork

Tastyworks claims that derivatives account for more than 90% of its customers' trades. Therefore, they naturally spend a lot of effort building tools for options and futures traders. Everything is set up to assist traders in determining volatility and profit potential. The entire Tastyworks platform is designed to help you make decisions and take action. Tastyworks only opened its virtual doors in 2017; therefore, it doesn't have the legacy systems that many older online brokers do. This has greatly aided it in limiting the options trading experience to the bare minimum. The Tastyworks platform relies heavily on watchlists, which are the same on mobile, online, and download. The mobile platform has a similar appearance and feels to the desktop versions, albeit there are pricing wheels and mechanisms to describe deals that reduce the risk of making a mistake.

A trade ticket is created for you to establish a position from a chart or a volatility screener. A video viewer is also included so you can keep an eye on the tastytrade network. Though a beginner to options trading may feel uneasy at first, individuals who are familiar with the fundamentals will appreciate the material, functionality, and concentration apparent throughout tastyworks platforms.

E*Trade

New options traders require assistance in knowing how trading derivatives might assist portfolio returns. The more advanced tools at E*TRADE are beautifully designed and will guide you through the process. In addition, the Power E*TRADE website and mobile app can assist you as you progress to options and derivatives.

The Power E*TRADE online and the app can be configured to display the functions you use most frequently, so you don't have to look for them. The platform contains all of the features that came with E*TRADE's acquisition of OptionsHouse technology, including many training tools for new options traders. The whole range of tradable assets is accessible on the mobile apps, and watchlists are connected throughout E*TRADE's platforms. The mobile apps provide very smooth functioning. We also discovered that utilizing Power E*TRADE on a tablet is a pleasurable experience.

eOption

For options transactions, eOption charges $1.99 for each leg, but the per-contract fee is much lower than its competitors, making it ideal for heavy options traders. eOption also offers commission-free stock and ETF trading, so people who prefer options and want low-cost access to other assets will be happy. In addition, customers are charged clearing and exchange costs, typically a fraction of a penny per share and detailed on the buy confirmation screen. eOption also received excellent ratings for its low margin rates.

CHAPTER 5

Tips and Good Habits

You must adopt an "investor" or "trader" mindset to make money in the markets. Here are some advantages of the availability and good practices to include in your daily routine.

Only put money at risk, which you can afford to give up

This is a precious guideline that must be observed. Don't spend money that you don't have on items like food, rent, or a loan. The risks also are severe enough without risking credit you can't lose on top of it. Also, if you go ahead, don't utilize the money that could cause a rift between you and your partner. If you want to make trades, professions and are still in the game after two years, consider yourself a great success. You're in the big leagues if you're making money at that time. Former traders who burnt themselves or their capital out are scattered throughout the trading and financial sector. Begin with reasonable expectations and a little amount of risk money. You'll be able to grow your risk capital as you make continuous progress steadily. According to the rule of thumb, never put more than five percent of your trading capital at risk on a specific contract., according to the rule of thumb. For accounts under $20,000, a 10% fee is acceptable.

Before you deal, make trading or fully funded and write it down in detailed and exact words.

A black-box system should not be confused with trading regulations. Instead, your trading strategy should be made up of a collection of implicit principles that you follow repetitively. You can modify these principles by general rules, variations, and permutations, but you should initially read them aloud and comprehend them. They're also useful to have on hand, especially while trading or making investment choices. A conceptual image can assist you in accomplishing this concisely and visibly. Brainstorming is essentially a sketch, such as a branching tree with the main trunk, in which the rules are represented using various colors and symbols rather than simply writing them down in a list.

Before you make any form of trade or even analysis, get into a relaxed state of mind

According to one estimate, psychology accounts for 80% of trading success. In contrast, technical competence accounts for 20%. I'm not sure how they came up with that figure, but the point is effectively stated. Regardless of your technical ability or expertise, your state of mind is critical to the future of your firm, and to do oneself credit; you should be in a better state of mind.

Please don't invest too much

You must only take on as many deals as you can handle without going insane. If you really can manage twenty deals at once while being calm, confident, and in command, that's fine. We're all different, and we deal in different ways. Find out what works best for you in terms of portfolio and time frame. Long-term investors may find that a larger portfolio is easier to manage. For shorter-term day trading, one or two live deals should sufficient.

Limit yourself to two to three tactics that you enjoy and that work for you

Only a few trading tactics are used by the world's best and most successful traders. Why complicate matters when there are so many factors to consider while making an investment decision? There are just three possible outcomes: the price will rise, fall, or remain unchanged. The only other factor to consider is the timeline, or how long does it take to increase or decrease, or how long will it remain static or price bracket? This is enough to think about without having to consider a variety of options. Different people prefer different tactics, which is why this book includes a variety. Keep going, and don't try to be too clever. Once you've figured out what you're comfortable with and are successful.

Don't fall in love with a stock or despise it, and don't become too tied to a job

One of the most important rules is this one. You do not earn money from stock. Your choice makes your point successful, and you only deposit that money when you exit that profitable position. Likewise, a share does not lose money, thus trying to also the score on a share in which you've already lost money is pointless. On the other hand, just because you've lost money with stock before doesn't mean you won't make money with it again if your requirements are met. The appropriate triggers are activated; of course, just because you've made money with stock before doesn't indicate you'll make money with it again. However, if you understand a stock's qualities and are willing to look at both up and down as valuable opportunities, you can boost your chances of success. Stocks, commodities, and all other securities are just buy-and-sell instruments. Some investors trade only one stock, index, futures contract, or resource at a time. This is OK because they are not locked to a position; instead, they use that asset as their preferred weapon for side-to-side trading.

Knowing and understanding your overall risk before making any options trading

Make sure you comprehend the risk, reward, and breakeven scenarios for the deal you're considering before making a trade, no matter how easy the options strategy is. Trade with your eyes open and the tools you'll need to succeed.

Keep a trade journal

Make it a practice to write down your investment strategies and the rationale behind them every day. You should write down the stock symbol, the way you believe it is moving, the reason for this, the historical and basic research that supports your judgment, and the expected time frame for the move. Make a note of the time, method, and any other relevant information that you believe may affect your decision-making abilities when you make a deal. Some dealers keep track of the weather, what they've eaten, and many other things to analyze their quality and help modifications to their trading approach.

Exchange visiting

Spend a day at an exchange to get a firsthand look at what happens. If you live in a wealthy financial hub, you have no excuse. It allows you to see what needs to happen for your order to be fulfilled. Everything presented here is a rudimentary grasp of market trends, not a complete thesis. Because occurrences in the open platform happen so quickly, you learn to appreciate that your exact move isn't disrupting the floor traders. Some day traders become concerned that the floor traders are plotting to locate their stops. Stop being anxious; it's not a healthy trading mindset to have.

Make a mental note of where you want to stop

Stop placement is both an art and a profoundly personal experience. Avoid the obvious point where everyone else is and position it a little further out, hopefully just out of reach of the knowledgeable locals. They will always swarm to a crowded city of stop orders. To put it another way, stay away from the gambling attitude when discipline is thrown out the window. Consider the case of a husband who returns home from the casino to his patient wife. He has promised her that if he gambles, he will only risk $100. Despite this, he returns home with his tail between his legs, humbly admitting that he has lost $1,000, only to exclaim excitedly, "But don't worry, honey, I'll win it all back tomorrow night." Be disciplined in all aspects of your trading, from analysis to entry, management, and eventually exit, to avoid becoming a gambler.

Avoid fighting the market when possible

Make sure you're not trading against the market if you want to make a directed trade. It carries greater weight than any individual stock. Always bear in mind what's going on in the larger market before joining your transaction.

It's preferable to lose a chance than it is to lose money

Don't be too hard on yourself if you miss out on a chance (the one that got away). You merely missed out on a chance; your bank account remained unharmed. It's pointless to be upset about it because you haven't spent, lost, or earned any money. If you saw a terrific chance but didn't take advantage of it, ask yourself why and at the very least give yourself credit for seeing it. On a daily basis, the market presents opportunities. First, you'll discover another one, and next, when you recall that it must meet your rules, you'll behave more confidently and with the advantage of past knowledge.

If you can play suggestions from friends, family, or friends of friends as a straddle, strangle, or fake call

Haven't we all taken a stock tip at some point? And haven't we also been burned by them? So, recognizing that we're all human and may be tempted to follow a hot tip again, let's discuss how to play them. For example, to trade a tip where you hold the shares plus a put option, only employ straddles, strangle, or fake call. Unfortunately, so many times, these dazzlingly vital bits of data end up going in the wrong direction and at an astounding rate.

Penny stocks and weak securities should be avoided

Don't be fooled into believing that a stock with a low price is necessarily a smart buy. Also, ensure that whatever you purchase can be sold. Volatility, in general, generates trade flows and a big disparity between the bid and ask. To avoid these assets, stick to equities with at least 500,000 average daily volume (ADV).

Forecasting should be avoided

Despite having access to more back-office and high-tech resources, analysts regularly mispredict stock direction. Regardless of the gloomy view that analysts' primary purpose is to obtain corporate clients rather than accurately anticipating price movements, it's vital that you don't make market predictions on a regular basis. Isn't the goal of trading and investing in the first place to create price estimates? You'd believe. That's a fantastic idea, but your primary focus is on responding swiftly to market data, whether it originates from the technical and fundamental study. It could simply be semantics, but if you're constantly making predictions for your pals, you risk altering your psychology and being obsessed with your own predictions, even if they're wrong. What you're aiming for is a truly pragmatic approach to trading, where you treat it like a business and use elevated trades.

Accept full accountability for your conduct

Always assume responsibility for a trade regardless of the circumstances, rain or shine. Even if your broker is counseling you, it is ultimately your money; thus, you must be accountable for clicking the button. Taking blame allows you to decide if you want to keep making good trades or modify any bad decisions or methods. Not only does this rule apply to trade, but it also applies to many other facets of life. Those who constantly blame other people or circumstances will never be able to address their difficulties. Since they acquit themselves of any power to change their situation in the first place, they have troubles.

Internet forums should be avoided, like the plague

The vast majority of message boards are dangerous places where inexperienced investors are deceived by "bashers" and "diggers" who have nothing else to do than promote or criticize a company. We all know that rapidly shifting emotions have no place in a serious investing or trading attitude, and message boards are no exception. Likewise, it would help if you avoided chat room forums like the plague since they are full of misinformation. They're visited by well-intentioned but highly emotional merchants at best, and at worst, they're phonies' nurseries.

Do some research on self-proclaimed geniuses and the instructors

The problem isn't that there's not enough trading knowledge out there. The problem is that there is just too much schooling, and much of it is ineffective. It is undeniably possible to acquire the essential understanding and skills to succeed as an investment or dealer. If you're fresh to this, remember that it didn't happen overnight, so you'll have to consider it a hobby. Discovering various ways with widely diverse merits could be a part of your journey. Finally, any mentor or instructor from whom you seek to learn must provide you with a reference. Find former or anyone who has studied your contents and ask them if they learned anything useful, if they used what they learned, and if the lectures were helpful.

Black-box systems don't work forever

To be clear, we're speaking to a system in which you, the user, are required to do nothing except follow the automated signals as a guide to making judgments. All black-box systems have a lot of fans. They usually work for a short length of time before stopping. The issue is that they are static in design and stiff in structure. This inhibits them from reacting to quick changes in the market effectively. Always remember to approach trading and investing as a business. This normally involves some action on the part of the person doing it. So, avoid anything that promises you can become a millionaire by doing nothing. This isn't to say that you need to be a theoretical physicist to understand it. You must, however, submit your own material, so be ready. You have the ability to do it, and the rewards are entirely up to you.

Sponsored content with faked results should be avoided

With news stories like the Easy Process to Unstoppable Earnings, many adverts and articles claim to have achieved unprecedented levels of success. However, there is always a catch. So far, the ridiculous ones have been that the so-called unrivaled devices have only been computed and then curve equipped with an optimization problem. Because we, as traders, do not have that advantage, a system that depends on the benefit of time is useless. Not only that, but look for fine print that says the system's "results" are only dependent on semi and disregard bid-ask spreads. That isn't the method to put a believable system to the test for any technique you choose to utilize; paper trading is a vital research tool. On the other side, paper trading must be carried out as if it were a genuine trade. This requires that you purchase at the ask and sell at the bid, pay the appropriate fees, and are entirely truthful with yourself.

Participate in physical activities

Trading and investing usually entail spending a significant amount of time in front of a computer. It's critical that you go out and about and get your blood circulating properly. Although it is not advised that you run marathons, you should get outdoor time even if you only take a walk. Or, at the very minimum, it will clean the thoughts. Some of the traders like fly fishing. It was merely to see what all the excitement was about and found out what the secret was. It was the fact that You can't really think about anything when you're doing something like jump because it's so engaging and needs so much focus. It's not appropriate to be rigid in this situation, but balance is a positive idea.

CONCLUSION

You can utilize options as one of several investment vehicles to develop a successful financial portfolio, but it will take some effort on your part. Options trading methods can be frightening, and they require a certain level of forethought to be profitable. The greatest option for trading advice for beginners is to prepare ahead of time. Learn about the stock market, look up local brokers, and enlist the help of your friends and family. As you begin trading options, these procedures will be quite beneficial. Options may be a highly valuable addition to even the most established financial portfolios when done properly.

CPSIA information can be obtained
at www.ICGtesting.com
Printed in the USA
LVHW010423180621
690564LV00004B/403

9 783985 567270